SCHIRMER'S LIBRARY OF MUSICAL CLASSICS

Compositions for the Piano

FRÉDÉRIC CHOPIN

Edited, Revised, and Fingered by

RAFAEL JOSEFFY

Historical and Analytical Comments by

JAMES HUNEKER

BALLADES	— Library	Vol.	31
→ CONCERTO No. 1 IN E MINOR (Two-Piano Score) —	"	"	1350
CONCERTO No. 2 IN F MINOR (Two-Piano Score) —	"	"	1351
FOUR CONCERT-PIECES			
Piano I (or Piano Solo) —	"	"	38
Piano II (reduction of orchestra accompaniment) —	"	"	1352
IMPROMPTUS —	"	"	1039
MAZURKAS —	"	"	28
NOCTURNES —	"	"	30
PRELUDES —	"	"	34
RONDOS —	"	"	1184
SCHERZI AND FANTASY —	"	"	32
MISCELLANEOUS COMPOSITIONS —	"	"	36
WALTZES —	"	"	27

G. SCHIRMER, *Inc.*

PIANO CONCERTO IN E MINOR

I

THE chronology of the two piano Concertos has given rise to controversy; the trouble arose from the F minor Concerto, it being numbered opus 21, though composed before the Concerto in E minor. The former was published April, 1836; the latter September, 1833. Both works derive from Hummel and Field. The passage-work is superior in design to that of the earlier masters, the general character episodical, but episodes of rare worth and originality. As Ehlert says: "*Noblesse oblige*—and thus Chopin felt himself compelled to satisfy all demands exacted of a pianist, and wrote the unavoidable piano Concerto. It was not consistent with his nature to express himself in broad terms. His lungs were too weak for the pace in seven-league boots, so often required in a score. The Trio and Sonata for piano and violoncello were also tasks for whose accomplishment Nature did not design him. He must touch the keys by himself without being called upon to heed the players sitting next him. He is at his best when, without formal restraint, he can create out of his inmost soul."

"He must touch the keys by himself." Here you have summed up the reason why Chopin never altogether succeeded in conquering the sonata-form or in impressing his individuality upon the masses. His was a lonely soul. George Sand knew this when she wrote: "He made an instrument speak the language of the infinite. Often in ten bars that a child might play he has introduced poems of unequalled elevation, dramas unrivalled in force and energy. He did not need the great material methods to find expression for his genius. Neither saxophone nor ophicleide was necessary for him to fill the soul with awe. Without church organ or human voice he inspired faith and enthusiasm." It might be objected that Beethoven, too, aroused a wondering and worshipping world without the aid of these two wind instruments; but it is needless cruelty to pick at Madame Sand's musical criticisms. She had received no technical education and had so little appreciation of Chopin's peculiar genius for the piano that she could write: "The day will come when his music will be arranged for the orchestra without change of the piano score"—which is disaster-inviting nonsense. Criticism has sounded Chopin's weakness when writing for any instrument but his own, when writing in any form but his own. His Nocturnes, two or three of them, have been arranged for the violin or 'cello, but the general result is not satisfactory. There has even been an opera entitled "Chopin," composed on themes from all of his works. Nevertheless Chopin will always spell piano, only that and nothing more.

In the E minor Concerto I think I best like the Romanza, though it is less flowery than the *Larghetto* of the F minor Concerto. The C sharp minor part is imperious, while the murmuring mystery of the close mounts to the imagination. The Rondo is frolicksome, tricky, genial and genuine music for the piano. It is true that the first movement is too long, too much in one set of keys, and the working-out section too much in the nature of a technical study. I see no reason for amending my views as to the original orchestration which suits the character of the piano part, colorless and slipshod as is this orchestration—said to have been made by Chopin's colleague, Franchomme the violoncellist. But that should not prevent one from admiring the Tausig version, first played in America by Rafael Joseffy. Rosenthal prefers the original version with the first long *tutti* curtailed; but he is hardly consistent when at the close of the Rondo he uses the Tausig interlocking octaves.

II

Mr. Krehbiel once wrote, in discussing the question of rescoring the Chopin Concertos: "It is more than anything else a question of taste that is involved in this matter, and, as so often happens, individual likings, rather than artistic principles, will carry the day." It is admitted by musicians that the orchestration of the two Concertos is meagre and conventional, not to say hackneyed. The *tutti* written in the pre-Beethoven style rob the piano part of some of its incomparable beauty, became a clog in Chopin's fancy, and have done more to prejudice musicians against Chopin than any other compositions he has written. That they were penned by Chopin is more than doubtful, as his knowledge of instrumentation was somewhat slender, and the amazing fact will always remain that, while his solo compositions are ever free and far removed from all that is trite, the orchestral part of his Concertos is uninteresting to a degree. In both, the opening *tutti* are lengthy and skim all the cream and richness of the solos that follow. Now the tone of the piano can scarcely vie with that of the orchestra, yet in the first movement of the E minor Concerto the plaintive solo of the first subject is played; the audience and pianist must patiently wait till the band is finished and then, an anti-climax, the piano repeats the story, but by comparison dwarfed and colorless. In the Tausig version of the E minor opening the *tutti* omits entirely the familiar version, contenting itself with the small recording subject in E minor that is afterwards played by the piano. Then follow the rich opening chords on the keyboard, and we are plunged into *medias res* without further ado.

The orchestral *tutti* before the piano enters in C major, is in the Tausig version very effective despite the dreaded trombones. It may be admitted that here we get a touch of "Die Meistersinger" color, which is—so the story runs—because Wagner himself had a finger in the Polish pie; certainly Tausig submitted the amended score to him for judgment. That much is history. The orchestral canvas is broadened, the tints brighter, deeper, richer and offering a superior background for the jewelled piano passage-work. The brass choir floats the staccato tone of the piano, lending to it depth and increased sonority. For example, take the horn pedal-point in E, which occurs in the middle of the Romanza, where the piano sounds the delicate crystalline chromatic *cadenza* for three bars only. What a happy stroke for Tausig to introduce brass. It floats the fairy-like progression and in an ethereal hue, though orthodox pianists will say it is not Chopin; which I grant. But the changes in this Concerto are effective, they in no sense mutilate the integrity of Chopin's ideas. Where there is a chromatic scale in unison Tausig breaks it into double-sixths and -fourths, or chordal figures which are not mere pyrotechnics, only "pianistic" and more brilliant. Tausig, if he did alter a few details, did not commit a sin against good taste. He of all piano *virtuosi* penetrated deeper into the meanings of the tone-poet, interpreting his music incomparably; whereas Liszt was often taken to task by Chopin for his altering original texts to suit his own taste. As regards the *coda* of the first movement in the E minor Concerto, Tausig simply takes the rather awkward trill from the left hand, giving it to the 'celli and contrabasso, while the piano plays the passage in unison. Most pianists, Rosenthal excepted, acknowledge that the trill in the original is distracting and not effective. The chromatic work at the end of this movement is broader and more *klaviermässig* than the older version, the piano closing at the same time with the orchestra, the audience not being compelled to listen to cadences of the Hummel type. The piano part of the second movement is hardly touched by Tausig; this Romanza could not be improved, but the orchestration is so delicately colored, so spiritualized, that even a purist cannot groan disapproval.

Against the new version of the Rondo the war of complaint is raised. "What, he dares to tamper with the very notes, introducing sixteenths where Chopin wrote eighths!" True, but what an improvement. How much livelier is the rhythm, how much more joyful and elastic, and when the piano enters it is with added zest we listen to its cheerful song. It is a relief, too, when the flute and oboe take up the theme, the piano contenting itself with a trill. The other changes in the solo part throughout this movement are an admirable task and are effective, though they are not easier to play than the original. But the Rondo loses none of its freshness, while it gains in tone and dignity. The octaves at the close disturb in a degree the euphony, adding in brilliancy, and in reality sound better with the Tausig instrumentation, because of its massiveness, than if played with only the fragile Chopin scoring. But in either case these octaves must be delivered with lightness, swiftness, clarity, otherwise they become distressingly monotonous, even cacophonous. If a Concerto is a harmonious relationship between the solo instrument and an orchestra, then the Tausig version of the E minor Concerto fulfills the idea. This holds good in the case of added accompaniments by Robert Franz to Händel, but best of all remains the fact that the Tausig version is more effective than the Chopin, and what pianist can resist such an argument! Mr. Krehbiel justly adds that Tausig's emendations have greatly added to "the stature of the Concerto."

James Huneker

First Concerto

in E minor

Edited and fingered by
Rafael Joseffy

Frédéric Chopin. Op. 11

* Carl Tausig made a new arrangement of this Concerto
Carl Tausig hat dieses Concert neu bearbeitet

espress.
II
p
tr
cresc.
cresc.
f
sf
sf
ff

II
sf
pp
p
p dolce
cantabile
p legatiss.
p
Ped.

II
cresc.
Ped.
f
sf
ff con forza
sfp

II
dim.
ff
II
sfp
II
p
II
II
sempre p
smorz.

I
ff
f
I
ff
f
I

I
p
espressivo
Ped.
fz
p
I
Ped.
legatissimo
I
fz
Ped.

I
stretto
p
a tempo
rit. pp
colla parte
pp
risoluto
staccato
con forza rit.
colla parte

a tempo
tranquillo
fz
p
I
sempre p
p
I
poco agitato
I
dim.
p

I
Ped.
cresc.
pp
pp

I
f
pp
I
con fuoco
fz
f
I
fz
cresc.
Ped.

I
fff
I
ff
dim.
cresc.
dim.
I
p cresc.
ff con forza

appassionato
p dolce
pp
con espressione
legato
p
espress.
I
I
I

I
con anima
cresc.
fz
I
con forza
stretto
appassionato
fz
p
I

I
fz
p
fz
legatissimo
stretto
fz
f agitato
pp
cresc.
stretto

a tempo
leggierissimo
fz riten.
fz
p
I
Ped.
colla parte
a tempo
poco cresc.
fz
p
riten.
a tempo
risoluto
f
colla parte
a tempo

sempre cresc.
I
sf
Ped.
f
p delicatissimo
cresc.
p

I
ben marcato
I
cresc.
I
sf
sf
sf
cresc.
f

I
sf
sf
p delicatissimo
Ped.
p
cresc.
I
I

I
I
sempre più cresc.
I

I
p
cresc.
sempre più cresc.
I
I

8
ff
(tr)
ben marcato
(segue)
tr
cresc.
fz
f
cresc.
I
Tutti
II
sf

II
sf
ff
p
cresc.
f
pp

dolce ed espressivo
Solo
I
leggieriss.
I
legatissimo

I
fz
leggiero
I
I

rall.
a tempo
risoluto
fz
I
a tempo
rall.
risoluto
I
fz
fz
I
fz
fz
fz

I
Ped.
fz
I
fz
I
fz

I
fz
Ped.
I
Ped.
I
Ped.

I
fz
Ped.
I
fz
fz
Ped.
I
fz
fz
Ped.

I
fz
I
fz
f
Ped.
I
cresc.
Ped.

I
f
Ped.
cresc.

I
cresc.
f
sempre più f
marc.

I
Ped.
dim.
fz
p
cresc.
ff

I
I
I
p
f
tr
cresc.
ff

I
p
f
cresc.
sf
ff
Solo

I
Ped.
I
p
stretto
a tempo
rit.
pp
I
Ped.

I
risoluto
staccato
con forza
rit.
tranquillo
a tempo
legatiss.
fz p
colla parte
I
I

I
Ped.
p
I
Ped.
I
Ped.

I
cresc.
f
pp
f
pp
I
I

I
cresc.
f
dim.
Ped.
cresc.
f
Ped.
p

I
ff
fz
fz
Ped.
Ped.
Ped.
I
rall.
a tempo
p
dolce con espressione
pp
Ped.
Ped.
Ped.
Ped.
I
Ped.
Ped.
Ped.
Ped.
Ped.
Ped.

* This variant is by Chopin; or it may be played as at first:
Diese Variante ist von Chopin; oder wie das erste mal:

I
stretto
sempr' stretto
tr
Ped.

* The 16th-notes *legatissimo*, the 8ths slightly *staccato*
Die Sechszehntel sehr gebunden, die Achtel leicht *staccato*

I
Ped.
segue
I
Ped.
I
Ped.
Ped.

I
Ped.
I
Ped.
I
Ped.

con fuoco
I
Ped.
fz
sf
sempre
più animato e cresc.

I
f
p
sempre più f
cresc.
rit.
fz
cresc.

a tempo
fz > p
cresc.
molto cresc.
etc.
f
p
8
ff
marcato
(segue)
tr
mf
I

* Tausig, omitting the deceptive cadence and the orchestral postlude, lets the solo instrument finish the movement.

Tausig lässt_ mit Hinweglassung des Trugschlusses und der Orchesternachspiels_ das Soloinstrument den Satz [beenden.

Romanze
Larghetto (♩= 76)
I
Larghetto (♩= 76)
pp legatissimo
sempre pp
Solo
cantabile
p
pp
sostenuto
f
p

Solo
I
legatissimo
cresc.
espressivo
pp dolcissimo
dolce

I
cresc.
Ped.
con espress.
leggieriss. e legatiss.
dim.
pp
p

I
f
dim.
p
Ped.
I
cresc.
con forza
I
fz p leggiero
dim.
dolcissimo

I
Ped.
dim. e rall.
pp delicatissimo e legatissimo
Ped. smorz.
pp
dim. e rall.
a tempo
rall.
a tempo
p legatiss.

I
p
leggieriss.
Ped. legato
sempre p
cresc.
con fuoco
fz p
dim.
Ped.
p
legatissimo
leggierissimo
cresc.
f
p

I
pp
agitato
f
p
Ped.
tr
I
I
con forza
f
dim.

sotto voce
p
I
Ped. il basso sempre legato
cresc.
con forza
cresc. appassionato
fz

I
Ped.
Ped.
Ped.
Ped.
Ped.
Ped.
Ped.
Ped.
Ped.
Ped.
Ped.
f
fz

I
Ped.
I
Ped.
leggieriss.
dim.
26
I
Ped.
smorz.
rall.
p

a tempo
leggieriss. dim. e rall.
I
rall.
pp
Tempo I°
p legatissimo
Tempo I°
un poco marc.
sempre leggierissimo

I
dim.
I
I

sempre legatissimo
I
Ped.
I

I
Ped.
dim.
p
I
poco rall. e smorz.
attacca
smorz.
attacca

Rondo

I
Ped.
legatissimo
p
rall.
legg.
a tempo

I
leggierissimo
dim.
rall.
p
Ped.
a tempo
rall.
a tempo
I
Ped.
a tempo
I
stretto
poco riten.
poco riten.

a tempo
legato
dim.
a tempo
I
II
cresc.
ff
p
ff
p
ff
p
cresc.

I
p leggierissimo dim.
poco rall.
ff
p
rall.
a tempo
fz
scherzando
a tempo
I
I
ff

II
p
ff
II
cresc.
I
ff risoluto
cresc.
pp
I
fz

I
f legato
p
cresc.
legato
I
f
p
cresc.
legato
I
f
p

cresc.
legato
p
f
cresc.

I
p dolce
Ped.
I
marcato
cresc.
f
I
fz
fp cresc.

I
fz
p
leggieriss.
legatissimo e dim.
rall.
rall.
a tempo
a tempo
pp leggiero

p dolce
I
I
I

I
I
poco stretto
I
pp
rall.
rall.
dim.

a tempo
I
a tempo
cresc.
tenuto

ten.
I
senpre legato
cresc.
Ped.
fz
cresc.
Ped.

I
f
Ped.
Ped.
p legatiss.
ben marcato
I
cresc.
I
cresc.

sempre più f
fz
Ped.
brillante
fz p
p
f
I

leggieriss.
p e legatissimo
p
f
p
f
dolcissimo

I
I
I
dim.
Ped.
*
poco rall.
poco rall.

a tempo
I
a tempo
rall.
f a tempo
rall.
a tempo
I
stretto
I

a tempo
dim.
legato
a tempo
rit.
cresc.
I
I
I

I
p
ff
p
cresc.
p leggiero
dim.
poco rall.
scherz.
Ped.
ff
p
rall.
a tempo
f
Ped. legato
a tempo

I
Ped.
ff
cresc.
p
sf

I
cresc.
dim.
ten.
fz
dim.
sempre più p
p
cresc.
I
I

I
Ped.
cresc.
fz

I
marcato
cresc.
fz p
f
marcato
f con fuoco

I
Ped.
cresc.
fz
f

I
fz p
Ped.
sempre p
I
I

I
Ped.
cresc.

I
cresc.
fz
p
sf
p legg.

dolcissimo
poco stretto
pp

I
rall.
a tempo
f
pp rall.
a tempo
I
f
cresc.
I
f brillante
ff
p

I
fz p
Ped.
f
p

I
sempre cresc.
Ped.
fz
riten.
dolce
sf
p riten.

a tempo
p leggiero
Ped.
a tempo
I
f
segue
veloce
fz
sf

* Tausig played the close in octaves (as given below), and many imitated him later. In his case this variant was justifiable to a certain extent, as he parallels the— often entirely altered— piano-part with a fuller orchestration.

Tausig spielte den Schluss in Oktaven wie folgt— was nachher von Vielen nachgeahmt wurde. Bei Tausig hatte diese Variante eine gewisse Berechtigung, da er den oft ganz veränderten Clavierpart mit einer volleren Orchestration Hand in Hand gehen lässt.

I
f
I
I

I
I
I
ff
ff
molto cresc.
fz
ff
Ped.